ANDREW JACKSON

THE PEOPLE'S PRESIDENT

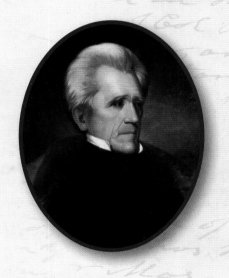

BECKON BOOKS

THE LAD ANDREW JACKSON AT THE WAXHAWS An illustration from *Sartain's* magazine imagines the attack of British troops on settlers in the Waxhaws during the Revolutionary War. A young boy—Andrew Jackson—stands in the foreground.

ELIZABETH "BETTY" HUTCHINSON JACKSON

Elizabeth and Andrew Jackson Sr. were part of a tide of Scots-Irish Protestants from the north of Ireland who immigrated to the colonies in the eighteenth century. Prompted by economic and religious issues, these migrants settled in the backcountry of Pennsylvania, Virginia, and the Carolinas. Elizabeth Jackson's five sisters and their families lived in the Waxhaw region with the Jacksons, giving them a network of family and friends. After the death of her husband, Elizabeth Jackson abandoned the struggling family farm to move in with her better-off sister. Elizabeth became the family's housekeeper and nursed her ailing sister. She continued as a caregiver by nursing soldiers during the Revolutionary War.

IN MEMORY OF
ELIZABETH HUTCHINSON
JACKSON
MOTHER OF
ANDREW JACKSON
PRESIDENT OF THE U.S. 1829–1837
WHO GAVE HER LIFE IN THE
CAUSE OF INDEPENDENCE
WHILE NURSING REVOLUTIONARY
SOLDIERS IN CHARLES TOWN
AND IS BURIED IN CHARLESTON
ERECTED BY
REBECCA MOTTE CHAPTER D.A.R.

BEGINNINGS

Born fatherless without money, land, or rank and orphaned at a young age, Andrew Jackson blazed his own trail by taking chances, bending rules, and meeting conflict with a determination that would define his life. Jackson was born on March 15, 1767, in the Waxhaws, an area with a large Scots-Irish community on the border of North and South Carolina. His parents, Andrew and Elizabeth, had emigrated from Ireland two years earlier with his two older brothers, Hugh and Robert. Jackson's father, for whom he was named, died shortly before he was born.

Andrew Jackson was just nine years old when the Declaration of Independence was signed and only thirteen when he and his brothers attended militia drills and served as messengers in the Revolutionary War. Having witnessed violent warfare in South Carolina, young Jackson wanted to fight back. The war, however, brought immense tragedy to the Jackson family. Jackson's oldest brother, Hugh, died of heatstroke after the Battle of Stono Ferry in 1779, and Jackson and his brother Robert were captured in 1781. During their captivity, a British officer slashed the young Jackson with his sword after he refused to polish the officer's boots.

Both Andrew and Robert contracted smallpox in prison. They were gravely ill when their mother arranged for their release in a prisoner exchange. Shortly after being set free, Robert succumbed to the illness. When Jackson was out of danger, his mother traveled to Charleston to aid the war effort by nursing injured and sick soldiers. While there, she contracted cholera and died, leaving Jackson without parents or siblings at the age of fourteen.

YOUNG MAN This miniature of a red-haired, blue-eyed young man is traditionally thought to be Jackson.

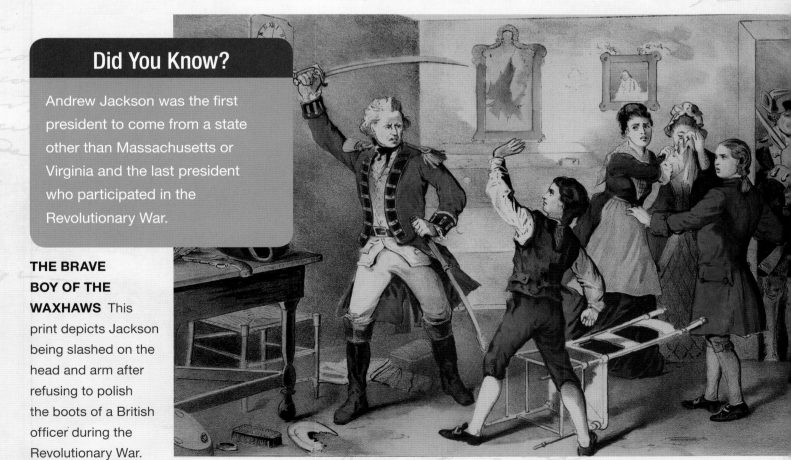

Did You Know?

Andrew Jackson was the first president to come from a state other than Massachusetts or Virginia and the last president who participated in the Revolutionary War.

THE BRAVE BOY OF THE WAXHAWS This print depicts Jackson being slashed on the head and arm after refusing to polish the boots of a British officer during the Revolutionary War.

After the death of his brothers and mother, Jackson briefly resided with members of his mother's family, but he soon left the Waxhaws for Charleston. Although he did not like formal studies, he read from the Bible and dozens of daily and weekly newspapers throughout his life.

In 1784, when he was seventeen, Jackson decided to become an attorney. He moved to Salisbury, North Carolina, where he studied law by apprenticing with prominent lawyers. After three years, he received his license to practice law. While living in North Carolina, Jackson gained a reputation for being charismatic, wild, and ambitious. He loved to dance, entertain, gamble, and spend time with friends in taverns.

Soon after Jackson turned twenty-one, the region's Superior Court judge appointed him as the prosecuting attorney for the newly formed Western District of North Carolina, which stretched from the Appalachian Mountains to the Mississippi River. Jackson moved to the Tennessee frontier and never looked back, seeing himself as a westerner for the rest of his life.

Andrew Jackson served in his first elected position as a delegate to the Tennessee Constitutional Convention in Knoxville in 1796. There, he helped draft Tennessee's first state constitution and bill of rights. That same year, Jackson was elected to serve as Tennessee's first member of the US House of Representatives (1796–1797). A year later, he was selected by the Tennessee General Assembly to serve as a US senator (1797–1798).

Due to impatience with the legislative process and mounting financial difficulties at home, Jackson cut his senatorial career short in 1798. He returned to Tennessee and was elected a judge on Tennessee's Superior Court. Jackson remained involved in politics and continued to correspond with important leaders such as President Thomas Jefferson.

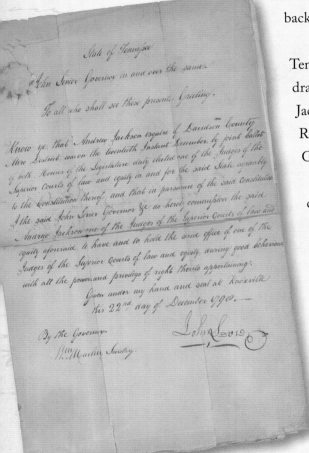

JUDICIAL COMMISSION Shortly after Tennessee Governor John Sevier signed this commission, Jackson began his term as a Superior Court judge.

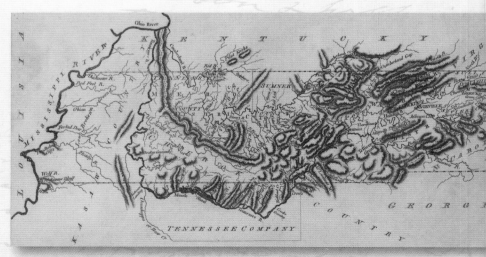

MAP OF TENNESSEE While a judge, Jackson ran businesses in Davidson and Sumner Counties, shown on this 1804 map.

Did You Know?

Jackson went to Charleston with a modest amount of money, and when it ran out, he worked as a schoolteacher for a short period of time.

THE HERMITAGE This rendering depicts the log farmhouse and kitchen as they likely appeared when the Jacksons lived in the farmhouse from 1804 to 1821.

JOHN OVERTON

A trusted friend and advisor to Andrew Jackson, John Overton was a Tennessee lawyer, jurist, banker, and political leader. Jackson and Overton worked together as young attorneys in the 1790s and became business partners in land speculation. In August 1804, Overton was elected to succeed Jackson as a member of the Superior Court of Tennessee, a position Overton held until 1810. Overton was one of Jackson's most fervent supporters and defenders, especially in the controversy surrounding Jackson's marriage. In the early 1820s, Overton helped organize the "Nashville Junto," a loose committee of Jackson's closest friends who planned and promoted his presidential campaign.

Generall Jackson and his Lady.

CELEBRATING COUPLE While this 1831 piece is not meant to be a likeness of the Jacksons, the artist, Reverend Henry Young, intended it to pay homage to Jackson's victory at the Battle of New Orleans.

RACHEL DONELSON JACKSON

Rachel was born in 1767 in Virginia. When she was twelve, her father led her family and a large group of others on a flotilla on the Tennessee and Cumberland Rivers. They traveled for nearly one thousand miles, arriving in Tennessee in 1780 to become some of the first white settlers of Nashville. They moved for a time to Harrodsburg, Kentucky, where Rachel married Lewis Robards before the family returned to Nashville. After her divorce from Robards and marriage to Andrew Jackson, Rachel became more religious. By her own admission, Rachel preferred the company of her family and church services to constant social engagements. She passed away unexpectedly shortly after Jackson was elected president, in December 1828.

MARRIAGE AND HONOR

After arriving in Nashville in 1788, Andrew Jackson boarded at the widow Rachel Stockley Donelson's station (a fortified family compound). He took a fancy to her vivacious daughter, also named Rachel. However, she was already married to Lewis Robards, a man nine years her senior. Rachel had lived with him only a short time, in Kentucky, before returning to her mother's home in Nashville. Though estranged, Robards came after Rachel. However, he left without her, infuriated with what he believed to be flirtation between Jackson and Rachel.

Jackson accompanied Rachel to Natchez in the Mississippi Territory in 1790. When they returned later that year, Jackson said they were married, though no record of this marriage survives today. In 1790, Robards began the divorce process, a difficult and lengthy procedure at the time. The divorce was finalized in 1793, with Robards charging Rachel with adultery and bigamy. Jackson and Rachel were officially wed on January 18, 1794.

After their wedding, Jackson pursued a career in politics. He then purchased a 420-acre plantation near Nashville in 1804 and named it The Hermitage. He and Rachel first resided in a well-built and nicely furnished two-story log farmhouse on the property. Once they moved into a new brick mansion in 1821, Jackson converted the farmhouse into single-story slave quarters.

Even after Jackson and Rachel were married and settled, Jackson maintained his reputation for being hot-tempered. In 1806, a quarrel with Charles Dickinson over a horse race turned violent when Dickinson allegedly made rude comments about Rachel's character. Jackson challenged Dickinson to a duel to defend his honor. Dickinson, a well-known marksman, fired the first shot, wounding Jackson in the chest. Despite this, Jackson took his shot, but the gun misfired. This counted as Jackson's returning shot, but he fired a second time, mortally wounding Dickinson. Jackson recovered from his injury after several months, but because of questions about Jackson's actions, his reputation was damaged.

IN MINIATURE This miniature (left) shows Jackson during his presidency, while the miniature of Rachel (right) was painted after her death.

"A being so gentle and virtuous, slander might wound but could not dishonor."

—INSCRIPTION ON RACHEL JACKSON'S TOMBSTONE

PRELUDE TO WAR

In 1800, the United States of America was still a fledgling nation, and it wasn't clear that it would ever master its own destiny. The British still ruled Canada, while Spain controlled modern-day Florida, Texas, and the Southwest.

In Jackson's mind, the United States was hemmed in by foreign interests. Many Americans shared Jackson's feelings regarding foreign nations, especially in regard to relations with Great Britain. During the early 1800s, Britain disrupted international trade by boarding American ships, seizing those they claimed were British crewmen, and forcing them into service with the Royal Navy, a practice called impressment. In addition, British blockades of European ports created hardships for Americans, especially southerners wanting to sell cotton.

These actions against the United States enraged a group of US politicians, including Senator Henry Clay and Representative John C. Calhoun, who became known as the "War Hawks."

IMPRESSMENT British-American relations declined when British ships impressed sailors off American vessels.

They became fiercely determined to declare war on Britain and, in so doing, expand American territory by capturing Canada.

When the United States declared war on Great Britain in the summer of 1812, Andrew Jackson had left politics, his social standing had fallen, and his finances were in shambles. Jackson found renewed hope in the opportunities the war with Britain offered for the future of the United States, as well as for him personally as general of the Tennessee militia, a post he had been elected to a decade earlier. Moreover, the war fed into his deeply ingrained need to prove himself.

BOXING MATCH This 1813 cartoon portrays Brother Jonathan (America) and John Bull (Britain) as boxing opponents.

JAMES MADISON

Even before becoming the fourth president of the United States (1809–1817), James Madison was a major political figure. He helped shape the US Constitution and frame the Bill of Rights, co-wrote the Federalist Papers, and enacted the first revenue legislation. As president, Madison faced intense pressure from the War Hawks to declare war on Great Britain in June 1812. The young nation, however, was not prepared to fight. American attempts to conquer Canada met disaster. In 1814, the British raided Washington, DC, setting fire to the White House and the Capitol.

EARLY PORTRAIT, 1817 There are no known official images of Andrew Jackson before the Battle of New Orleans. Painted by Ralph E. W. Earl in 1817, this is one of the earliest portraits of Jackson.

With the expansion of US territory, more frequent disputes with Native Americans occurred. In 1811, the United States defeated an Indian confederation at the Battle of Tippecanoe; afterward, Shawnee Chief Tecumseh formed an alliance with the British, convinced that it was the Shawnees' only hope to secure the Northwest Territory. This added to mistrust of Indians and the resentment the United States held toward Great Britain and its interference in American matters.

BOLD VICTORY Images of the Battle of New Orleans were stock-in-trade for makers of popular prints for years afterward. This illustration shows General Jackson and his officers behind the cannon.

"These brave men, at the call of their country, voluntarily rallied. . . . They followed me to the field; I shall carefully march them back to their homes."

—ANDREW JACKSON TO GENERAL JAMES WILKINSON, MARCH 22, 1813

BECOMING OLD HICKORY

Despite his lack of formal training as a soldier, Andrew Jackson was elected general of the Tennessee militia in 1802. In late 1812, Jackson and the Tennessee militia were ordered to Natchez in the Mississippi Territory to prepare for a British invasion of New Orleans. But supplies and food were scant, and many of Jackson's troops fell ill.

When the threat of invasion passed, Jackson received orders to disband his troops and let them find their own way home through hostile Indian territory. Instead, Jackson led them back himself, at times giving up his own horse so the sick could ride. Jackson's toughness and determination reminded his troops of tough hickory wood, earning him the nickname "Old Hickory."

A year later, Jackson caught the nation's attention by delivering the final blow to end the Creek War. The Creek War began as a civil war between two factions of the Creek Nation in Georgia and Alabama. While some Creeks (the White Sticks) encouraged assimilation into white culture, others (the Red Sticks) held a more traditionalist view and advocated war against the whites.

In August 1813, the Red Sticks attacked Fort Mims near Mobile, Alabama, killing about 250 people, including women and children. Andrew Jackson and his Tennessee militia mobilized in response to the massacre, with Cherokees and White Sticks riding with him.

Jackson's militia fought the Red Sticks in a series of battles in northern Alabama. Finally, on March 27, 1814, Jackson's army surrounded them at Horseshoe Bend and inflicted a punishing defeat, effectively ending the war. Jackson's determined leadership during the Creek War and in the War of 1812 would lead to a presidential commission as major general in the United States Army.

PERFECT LIKENESS
The unknown sculptor of this marble bust copied William Rush, whose original bust was said to be a perfect likeness of Jackson.

BATTLE OF HORSESHOE BEND In the last battle of the Creek War, the Red Sticks barricaded themselves behind a dirt and log wall across a narrow bend in the Tallapoosa River. The barricade was nearly impervious, but American troops later crossed the river behind the Red Sticks and inflicted massive casualties.

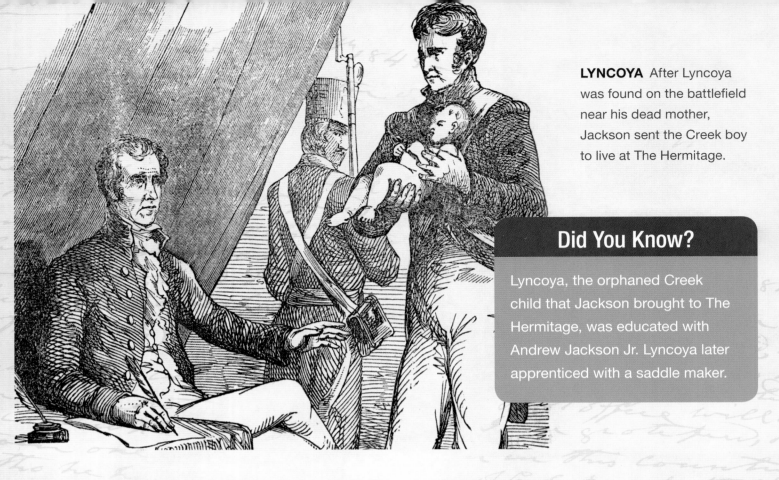

LYNCOYA After Lyncoya was found on the battlefield near his dead mother, Jackson sent the Creek boy to live at The Hermitage.

Did You Know?

Lyncoya, the orphaned Creek child that Jackson brought to The Hermitage, was educated with Andrew Jackson Jr. Lyncoya later apprenticed with a saddle maker.

MIGHTY SWORD General Jackson carried this sword and scabbard while commanding his Tennessee and American troops during the Creek War and the War of 1812.

THE CREEK INDIANS

The early 1800s were a time of change and unrest for the Creek Indians. Some wanted to assimilate to white culture. Others (the Red Sticks) felt the tribe should follow the religious teachings of Tenskwatawa, "the Prophet," who called for a return to traditional ways. This conflict resulted in civil war. In 1813, the United States' anxiety over Creek relations with Spain and Britain, as well as the Red Sticks' attack at Fort Mims, led to war against the Red Sticks. After the Battle of Horseshoe Bend, Jackson imposed treaties on the Creek Nation, forcing them to cede twenty-three million acres to the United States.

THE HERO OF NEW ORLEANS This image by Nathaniel Currier inspired countless Jackson tributes. Most characterized Jackson as the larger-than-life hero of a ragtag fighting force.

A NATIONAL HERO

With his commission as major general in the US Army in 1814, Andrew Jackson was charged with defending the 7th Military District (Tennessee, Louisiana, and Mississippi Territory). He entered New Orleans on December 1, 1814, to strengthen its defenses against another rumored British invasion and meticulously prepared to lead the defense of New Orleans in what would become one of the most pivotal battles of the war.

Due to slow communications, neither the American nor the British forces were aware that negotiators in Belgium had signed the Treaty of Ghent on December 24, 1814, to end the War of 1812. Yet despite being signed, the treaty didn't actually become binding until February 16, 1815, once it had been ratified by both nations.

At dawn on January 8, 1815, British troops mounted a direct assault on Jackson's lines. The Americans were inexperienced and poorly armed and equipped compared to the British troops, however, American cannon and musketry overwhelmed the British soldiers within minutes. More than two thousand British troops were killed or wounded, while Jackson lost only seventy-one men. Against all odds, Andrew Jackson and the Americans had defeated troops from one of the world's best professional armies.

The news of Jackson's victory at New Orleans and the ratification of the Treaty of Ghent set off a wave of celebration and national pride. Americans heralded Jackson as the man who finally delivered a glorious conclusion to a long and difficult war. In defeating the British, he had restored the nation's dignity and had proven, beyond all doubt, that America was here to stay.

WAR OF 1812 MEDAL Congress awarded Jackson a gold medal after the Battle of New Orleans.

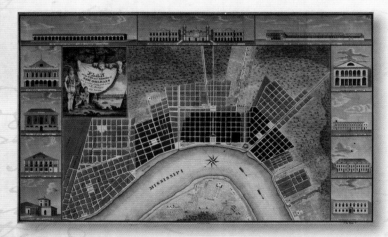

MAP OF NEW ORLEANS, 1815 Jackson established headquarters at 106 Royal Street, near the Cathedral of Saint Louis and the Place d'Armes.

JACKSON'S ARMY

Andrew Jackson had just a few weeks to transform a diverse group of men into a cohesive, disciplined fighting force. Over two thousand were militia from Kentucky and Tennessee, armed with a motley assortment of muskets and rifles and some not armed at all. A notorious French pirate, Jean Lafitte, and his Baratarians chose to join Jackson's army in exchange for a pardon. A small number of Choctaw warriors also decided to align with Jackson rather than support the British army. In addition, Jackson assigned two battalions of Creole-born "free negro" militia to his defense, angering many white Americans.

"All the boasted preparation, which the British government has been making . . . , is about to terminate in a final blow against New Orleans."
—JAMES MONROE TO ANDREW JACKSON,

Did You Know?

The Treaty of Ghent effectively negated any gains made by the Americans or the British, restoring all borders to their location before war was declared in the summer of 1812.

PRIZED POSSESSION The mayor and aldermen of New York presented this gold box to Jackson in 1819 for his military service in the War of 1812. It was one of his most cherished possessions.

OFFICIAL COMMISSION After the Creek War, Andrew Jackson—who had been major general of the Tennessee militia—was commissioned a major general in the US Army.

After the Battle of New Orleans, the American people couldn't get enough of Andrew Jackson. Over three long years, the British had inflicted a series of humiliating defeats. Yet in one swift blow, Jackson's victory made Americans feel that all that had been reversed. Jackson's face appeared everywhere—on coins and medals, plates and pitchers, handkerchiefs and silk ribbons. State and local governments lauded him with presentation gifts, including swords and a gold box, while the United States awarded Jackson the Congressional Gold Medal.

MILITARY PORTRAIT Jackson's victory at the Battle of New Orleans created great demand for portraits of him.

BATTLE OF NEW ORLEANS This view of Chalmette Plain shows the Americans' advantage over British forces. A Louisiana militiaman painted this scene based on sketches made after the battle.

Jean Hyacinthe de Laclotte. *Battle of New Orleans*, New Orleans Museum of Art: Gift of Edgar William and Bernice Chrysler Garbisch, 65.7

CONFIDENT LEADER Most renderings of Andrew Jackson, including this one based on a Thomas Sully portrait, depict a military leader full of ability, vigor, and confidence.

"Jackson loved progress. He liked the idea of the United States expanding geographically, developing economically, and of Americans acquiring greater and greater material prosperity."

—DANIEL FELLER, PROFESSOR OF HISTORY, UNIVERSITY OF TENNESSEE, AND EDITOR/DIRECTOR, *THE PAPERS OF ANDREW JACKSON*

CREATING AN AMERICAN EMPIRE

For years, Andrew Jackson complained that Washington was failing to protect the areas west of the Appalachians from Indian and foreign interests. In his eyes, the southern United States suffered from two security problems: Native Americans and Spanish Florida.

Jackson used his reputation as a fierce fighter and the threat of force to get the Creeks, Chickasaws, Cherokees, and Choctaws to sign treaties ceding huge tracts of land to the United States. For Native Americans, these accords proved disastrous and were the first step in their eventual removal west.

Jackson believed Spanish Florida also threatened American security due to America's lack of military power in the region. The British saw Florida as a possible route of invasion, and the Seminole tribe often carried out raids in the United States, then fled to Spanish Florida. In 1818, Jackson, under orders to cross into Florida to subdue the Seminoles, went further and attacked and conquered two Spanish garrisons. After three months, Jackson declared the Seminole threat over and withdrew.

Spain realized that Jackson and the United States were determined to take Florida, and negotiations opened in 1819. Hesitantly resigning from the US Army, Jackson became the governor of the new Florida Territory in June 1821. He quickly became disillusioned with the unending appointments and office seekers, the issues with the transition of the territory from Spain, and the political disagreements with President Monroe's administration. Andrew Jackson resigned the governorship in November and returned to The Hermitage in poor health. Rachel prayed that this time, he was home for good.

OSCEOLA An influential leader of his tribe, Osceola would again incite Seminole resistance against the United States during Jackson's second term as president.

THE SPANISH EMPIRE

In the 1700s, the Spanish Empire was the largest in the world and held a significant amount of land in the Americas. The empire began to unravel when the French, under Napoleon, acquired the Louisiana Territory. Napoleon's sale of the Louisiana Territory to the United States in 1803 caused border disputes between the United States and Spain. Meanwhile, Jackson's aggressive approach to Florida enabled Secretary of State John Quincy Adams to negotiate the Adams-Onís Treaty in 1819 from a position of strength. Adams arranged the cession of Florida, and Spain also relinquished its claim to the Pacific Northwest.

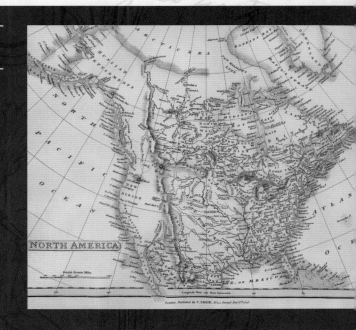

A NEW FIGHT

From 1812 to 1821, Andrew Jackson's military career made him a national hero and brought him increased wealth and opportunities. His countrymen saw him as a new leader, free from the corruption of the privileged political elite. In 1822, the Tennessee Legislature nominated him as a candidate for president of the United States. To test Jackson's political strength, he was nominated and elected as a US senator from Tennessee in 1823.

Jackson used his time in the Senate to make friends and political allies while also convincing Washingtonians that he was not an uncivilized westerner or military tyrant. His opponents soon discovered he wasn't an uneducated hothead but a pragmatic, strategic politician—and a serious political threat.

Jackson's tenure in the capital reinforced his belief that many politicians and government officers were corrupt. Nearly every week, some new Washington scandal was reported in the newspapers. Self-interested men were distorting the Founding Fathers' ideals, thought Jackson, and no one was doing anything to stop it.

When Americans went to the polls in 1824, the field consisted of three Washington insiders—John Quincy Adams, Henry Clay, and William H. Crawford—and Andrew Jackson. Although Jackson received the most popular votes, no candidate won the majority of the electoral votes, sending the decision to the House of Representatives. On February 9, 1825, the House elected John Quincy Adams as president.

Jackson graciously accepted defeat until rumors swirled that House Speaker Henry Clay and Adams had struck a deal to ensure Adams's election. When Adams named Henry Clay as his secretary of state, it confirmed Jackson's suspicions that the two men had reached a corrupt bargain, depriving the American people of their popular choice for president. Disheartened, Jackson resigned his Senate seat and returned to Tennessee. He and his supporters immediately began laying the groundwork for his election in 1828.

COFFIN HANDBILL Jackson's opponents in the 1828 election reminded voters that he had six militiamen—represented by these coffins—executed for desertion during the Creek War.

JACKSON'S FOES Jackson's relationship with Congress members Daniel Webster (middle) of Massachusetts and Henry Clay (right) of Kentucky was full of animosity.

ICONIC JACKSON Thomas Sully's 1845 portrait of Andrew Jackson, which most Americans recognize as the source for the image used on the $20 bill, depicts him as a vigorous president.

JOHN QUINCY ADAMS

John Quincy Adams, son of President John Adams, was born into America's political aristocracy. As secretary of state under President James Monroe, Adams was a skillful diplomat and negotiator. He was the sixth president of the United States from 1825 to 1829, proposing national programs of public works and establishment of a national university. Jackson's supporters labeled President Adams an elitist who engaged in backroom politics and was out of touch with the common man. In Congress, Jackson's men opposed Adams and his programs. By the end of his term, Adams had accomplished little due to opposition from Jackson, corruption in his administration, and his own shortcomings.

THE COUNTY ELECTION In this scene by George Caleb Bingham, diverse citizens take part in the democratic process. Jackson's era was characterized by universal white male suffrage, and public elections tended to be raucous affairs with voters calling out their choices in large gatherings.

ON DISPLAY
Based on an iconic image of Jackson from the 1828 campaign, this painting was likely created for display at a political rally or dinner.

By 1828, laws governing presidential elections were changing as more states allowed voters—not the state legislatures—to directly elect the electors and a greater number of voters cast ballots. However, there were restrictions on who could vote. Women could not vote in any state, and two-thirds of the states had restrictions on free African American voters, while slaves were not allowed to vote anywhere.

> *"The opinion of those whose minds were prepared to see me with a Tomahawk in one hand, & a scalping knife in the other has greatly changed."*
>
> **—ANDREW JACKSON TO GEORGE W. MARTIN, JANUARY 2, 1824**

PRESIDENTIAL JACKSON James Barton Longacre sketched this image of Jackson in 1829, early in his presidency, and then turned it into a popular engraving.

Did You Know?

As his outrage at the corruption of the Washington elite grew, Jackson began writing what he called "memorandoms," letting his anger spew out into them and the letters he sent to friends. Some were little more than angry tirades, but Jackson's political philosophy increasingly reached a broader audience.

PRESIDENT'S LEVEE Of Jackson's inauguration, Margaret Bayard Smith wrote, "Ladies fainted, men were seen with bloody noses and such a scene of confusion took place as is impossible to describe."

THE DEMOCRATIC PARTY

The Democratic Party grew out of the old Jeffersonian Democratic Republican Party. With the demise of the opposing Federalists by 1820, nearly every leading politician claimed to be a Democratic Republican. During the course of the Adams and Jackson administrations, the Democratic Republicans diverged into two groups: the National Republicans, led by John Quincy Adams and Henry Clay, and the Democrats, led by Andrew Jackson and Martin Van Buren. The National Republicans merged into the Whig Party in the mid-1830s. The Democratic Republicans dropped the Republican label during Jackson's presidency (1829–37) and called themselves simply Democrats or Jacksonian Democrats.

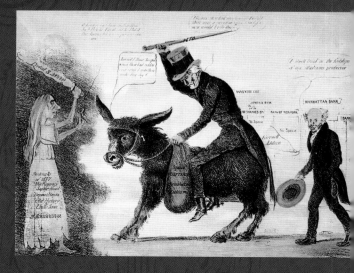

THE PEOPLE'S PRESIDENT

Even before President John Quincy Adams could deliver his first message to Congress in December 1825, the Tennessee Legislature had nominated Andrew Jackson to be the next president of the United States.

The campaign of 1828 was a nasty affair. Incumbent John Quincy Adams and his supporters criticized Jackson's military record—notably, his propensity for vicious discipline and his habit of ignoring the orders of his civilian superiors—as proof of his tendency to revoke people's rights. They also seized on his marriage to Rachel as an example of his immorality. But the Jackson camp matched Adams, stroke for stroke. Adams proved an easy target with his aristocratic bearing and administration tainted with corruption.

Jackson's message to voters was clear: He would return to the values of the Founders and limit the federal government to its constitutional obligations. He would get rid of the political insiders who abused their positions for personal gain, and he would protect individual liberty and give the common man a voice. Voters overwhelmingly elected Jackson. His victory was seen as a complete repudiation of Adams and his vision for America.

Soon after the election, jubilation turned to grief. Rachel Jackson died suddenly, on December 22, 1828. Despite his heartache, Andrew Jackson was determined to fulfill his role as the "people's president." Jackson supporters from across the nation flooded in to witness his inauguration, much to the dismay of the Washington elite. After Supreme Court Chief Justice John Marshall administered the oath of office, Jackson faced the crowd and bowed. As president of the United States, Andrew Jackson had signaled to his fellow Americans and the world that he was now the servant of the people.

LIBERTY TREE This sculpture portrays Jackson and King Louis Philippe after the French government paid claims to the United States in 1836—one of Jackson's foreign policy triumphs.

Did You Know?

During Andrew Jackson's presidency, his critics sometimes portrayed him as a jackass in political cartoons. Years later, cartoonist Thomas Nast adopted the donkey as a symbol of the Democratic Party, which endures today.

UNIQUE GIFT After Jackson received a 1,400-pound wheel of cheese, he hosted a public party on the White House lawn in February 1837. In two hours, the cheese was gone.

SAM PATCH Artist Ralph E. W. Earl portrays Andrew Jackson on his horse, Sam Patch. Jackson received the horse while on a goodwill tour of the northeastern United States.

"*He wanted sincerely to look after the little fellow who had no pull, and that's what a President is supposed to do.*"

—HARRY TRUMAN, *WHERE THE BUCK STOPS: THE PERSONAL AND PRIVATE WRITINGS OF*

Jackson Democratic Ticket
President
Andrew Jackson
Vice President
John C. Calhoun
ELECTORS
Ethan A. Brown, Hamilton co.
Robert Harper, Ashtabula
1 William Piatt, Hamilton
2 James Shields, Butler
3 Henry Barrington, Miami
4 Thomas Gillespie, Green
5 Thomas L. Hamer, Brown
6 Valentine Keffer, Pickaway
7 Robert Lucas, Pike
8 John M'Elvain, Franklin
9 Samuel Herrick, Muskingum
10 George Sharp, Belmont
11 Walter M. Blake Tuscarawas
12 Benjamin Jones, Wayne
13 William Rayen, Trumbull
14 Hugh M'Fall, Richland

In the 1820s, candidates didn't travel the country to campaign or appear at public rallies unless they lived nearby. Instead, they used the power of the newspaper—and their personal contacts. Candidates wrote letters outlining their ideas to friends in other states. If those contacts liked the candidates' ideas, they set up committees, staging rallies and speeches to drum up support. Jackson's committees called themselves "Hickory Clubs," a nod to Jackson's nickname, Old Hickory.

1828 DEMOCRATIC TICKET During the 1828 election, John C. Calhoun ran as Jackson's vice president. The two used the slogan "Jackson, Calhoun and Liberty."

OATH OF OFFICE Accompanied by War of 1812 veterans and his personal staff, Andrew Jackson was sworn in to office by Chief Justice John Marshall on March 4, 1829.

"*Jackson is to be President. and you will be HANGED.*"

YOU WILL BE HANGED Jackson's foes, who called him a tyrant, supported their accusations by recalling events such as this execution during the Seminole War.

COMMEMORATING A HERO To Americans, Jackson was the hero of New Orleans long before he became president of the United States. Items commemorating the battle (like this plate) were often used as campaign paraphernalia during the election of 1828.

EAST ROOM The East Room of the White House was first decorated during Jackson's presidency. He purchased furniture from Philadelphia cabinetmakers and wallpaper from France.

ELECTION OF 1824 This image of Andrew Jackson fighting off mongrel dogs forms a critical commentary on his treatment during the 1824 presidential election.

THE WHIG PARTY

The Whig Party was formally organized in 1834, bringing together a loose coalition of groups united in their opposition to Andrew Jackson's policies and use of executive power. Jackson's bank war and his opposition to nullification in South Carolina brought fiscal conservatives and proponents of southern states' rights together with those who still believed in the National Republican program of a protective tariff and federally financed programs and improvements. Because these groups were at first allied only by their dislike of Jackson, the Whigs had difficulty developing a unifying party platform. Their last candidate for president, Millard Fillmore, ran unsuccessfully in 1856.

CABINET CONFLICT

Andrew Jackson's time as president marked a major historical shift for the United States. Unfortunately, the first two years of his term were marred by a social scandal that turned political. Soon after the inauguration, a group of Washington women refused to socialize with Margaret Eaton, wife of Secretary of War John Eaton, because of rumors about her reputation. Such social slights spawned chaos in Jackson's Cabinet. He pleaded with his Cabinet members to get their wives to relent. In Margaret Eaton's treatment, he saw Rachel's situation all over again, and he wasn't about to let the issue drop. In addition, John Eaton had defended Rachel vigorously during the 1828 campaign.

During the so-called "Eaton Affair" or "Petticoat War," Jackson came to suspect that several Cabinet members were more loyal to Vice President John Calhoun than to him, and that Calhoun was planning to succeed him after only one term. Jackson became determined to run again himself, and he began to look to Secretary of State Martin Van Buren, rather than Calhoun, as his eventual successor.

EATON NOTE Designed like a note from the "Petticoat National Bank," this 1832 cartoon mocks the Eaton Affair.

By 1831, Jackson's administration was approaching paralysis, with Cabinet members barely on speaking terms. To cut the knot, Van Buren and Eaton offered to resign, giving Jackson a pretext to clear out the others as well and start over with a clean slate. Meanwhile, Jackson had come to rely mainly on a group of unofficial advisors for policy advice. His opponents labeled this group his "Kitchen Cabinet" because of its back door access to the president.

Did You Know?

Although Martin Van Buren resigned, Jackson included him in his unofficial Kitchen Cabinet, along with newly appointed Attorney General Roger Taney, Treasury auditor Amos Kendall, and newspaper editor Francis Preston Blair.

IMAGINATIVE RECEPTION This cartoon shows Jackson and his Cabinet entertaining popular French dancer Madame Celeste, suggesting they were easily distracted from governing.

OH RATS! This 1831 cartoon vividly renders the Eaton scandal, showing Jackson's Cabinet members to be wildly scattering rats. Jackson attempts to catch the rats by stomping on their tails.

MARGARET EATON

Margaret O'Neale Timberlake Eaton was a beautiful woman with a dubious reputation. The daughter of a boardinghouse keeper, she was said to have started an affair with John Eaton before her first husband died. Washington's political insiders not only took issue with this alleged behavior, but also with the special favor that Jackson showed to her and her husband. The ladies of Washington were scandalized that Margaret Eaton had suddenly risen to the height of Washington's social ladder. When Jackson forced the resignations of nearly his entire Cabinet, the Eaton Affair became national news.

GREAT FATHER This circa 1835 cartoon mocks Jackson's belief that he was acting in the best interests of native people he did not consider wise enough to make their own decisions.

"[The Indians] and my white children are too near each other to live in harmony and peace. . . . Their father has provided a country large enough for them all."

—ANDREW JACKSON TO DAVID W. HALEY, OCTOBER 15, 1829

A DEVASTATING DECISION

From the nation's founding, the United States had created formal policies governing Indians. Most were designed to encourage Native Americans to assimilate into the white or "civilized" population. Formal treaties guaranteed the Indians the right to stay on ancestral lands east of the Mississippi River and govern themselves. Still, white settlement gradually pushed them west.

Many believed that assimilation of Native Americans was not possible, and the only way to avoid conflict and allow Indians to maintain self-rule and preserve their cultural identity was to remove them to federal lands west of the Mississippi. Andrew Jackson was a proponent of this policy.

President Jackson proposed the Indian Removal Act, which Congress passed in 1830 by a small margin after intense debate. Although the controversial law did not order the physical removal of Indians, it made their removal US policy and authorized the president to negotiate treaties to relocate them. The law also agreed to cover all costs for the Indians' travel and resettlement.

The federal government put pressure on tribes by refusing to protect them from settlers moving onto their lands and by using bribery to coerce treaties. Andrew Jackson signed over sixty land cession agreements, which moved nearly fifty thousand Indians westward, many to present Oklahoma. Some Indians went willingly. Others were forced.

Though he had railed against government corruption in the past, Jackson actively encouraged the shady treaties forced upon the tribes and the corruption of government officials. The Indian Removal process was largely completed within two years after Jackson left office with great loss of Native American life.

Today, Jackson's Indian Removal Act and its tragic consequences are a conspicuous blight on his legacy.

TRIBAL CULTURE As the Indian removals took place, artists portrayed members of various tribes with great dignity.

TRAIL OF TEARS
Only one of many removals from the eastern states, the Cherokees suffered from starvation, disease, exposure, and exhaustion on their "Trail of Tears."

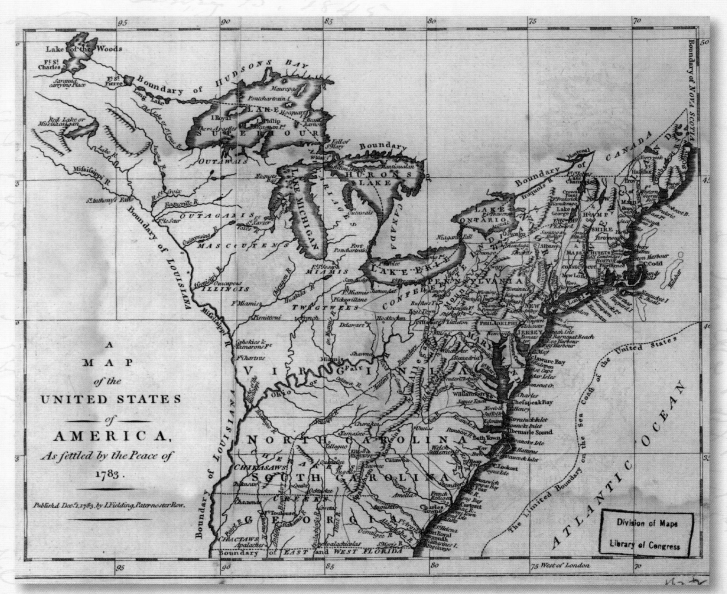

UNITED STATES MAP, 1783 This map shows the general locations of Indian tribes east of the Mississippi immediately after the Revolutionary War.

THE CHEROKEE INDIANS

In the 1820s, after decades of encouraged assimilation, many Cherokees became planters, and a group of mixed-race Cherokees rose to leadership to try to meet the American government on more equal footing. In 1827, they converted the tribe to a constitutional republic. John Ross was elected principal chief of the newly established Cherokee Nation in 1828. After the Indian Removal Act was signed in 1830, a few leading Cherokees concluded that only cooperation with the US government would ensure the tribe's survival. Without authority from Ross, these other Cherokee leaders signed the Treaty of New Echota in 1835 arranging for the tribe's relocation to Oklahoma.

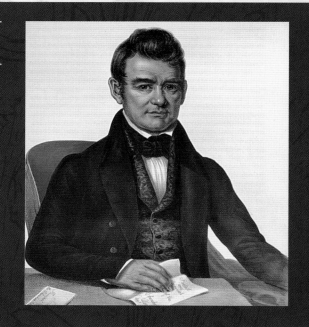

The discovery of gold deposits on Cherokee land in northern Georgia brought a flood of prospectors in 1829. Within months, thousands of miners overran the region and began digging mines, diverting streams, and building primitive mining camps, adding to the tensions already building between whites and Indians. These tensions aggravated federal-state conflicts over Indian policy. Georgia asserted that the state had jurisdiction over the Indian lands but federal policy treated the Indians as sovereign nations.

TATSI Led by Tatsi, Cherokees who moved west before the Indian Removal Act were called "Old Settlers."

A NORTHERN TRIBE MOVES This image shows the Potawatomi people, led by Chief Kee-wau-nay, signing over land in Indiana to the United States in 1837. They termed their removal process the "Trail of Death."

Glenn A. Black Laboratory of Archaeology at Indiana University, Bloomington

CHECKS AND BALANCES

Andrew Jackson believed that since the president was elected by "all of the people," he was the only member of government who represented "all of the people." During his two terms as president, he asserted powers that no president had before. President Jackson used his veto power to block major legislation, such as road and canal bills and the renewal of the charter of the Second Bank of the United States in 1832. Presidents before Jackson had vetoed bills rarely and reluctantly. Jackson established a new practice of using the veto as an instrument of policy.

Jackson also exercised his executive power during the crisis with South Carolina, led by Jackson's vice president, John C. Calhoun. South Carolinians felt the present tariff (tax on imports) was both oppressive and unconstitutional, since it used the federal government's taxing power to promote northern manufacturing at their expense by raising the price of cheaper foreign goods. Calhoun advanced the idea that a state was the ultimate interpreter of the constitution and had the right to nul-

State-Rights & Nullification
TICKET.
FOR STATE CONVENTION.

SAMUEL E. NELSON,
THOMAS G. M'FADDEN,
JOHN L. FELDER,

ONE-WAY TICKET South Carolina declared the Tariffs of 1828 and 1832 unconstitutional and unenforceable by a state convention vote of 136 to 26.

lify (or invalidate) any federal law it deemed unconstitutional. He also believed that states could secede from the Union.

In late 1832, South Carolina nullified the Tariff of 1832 and threatened secession. Jackson rejected this action and promised to use force if South Carolina disobeyed the law. After much maneuvering, Congress passed a compromise tariff that placated South Carolina and a bill that authorized the use of force against nullification. Jackson's actions prevented a break in the Union, as well as setting precedents that Abraham Lincoln would later use to oppose secession.

US CAPITOL This print shows the Capitol building in 1829, at the beginning of Jackson's presidency.

IN HIS TIME

During the Jackson administration, there was no shortage of conflict, not the least of which concerned states' rights. Jackson, like many Americans, believed strongly in every state's right to determine what happened within its borders and to its people. But when a state's laws and interests collided with federal laws and interests, as it did with South Carolina, Jackson came down firmly on the side of the Union and the people who created it.

"Our federal union, it must be preserved!"

—ANDREW JACKSON, IN A TOAST AT THE ANNUAL THOMAS JEFFERSON BIRTHDAY DINNER, APRIL 13, 1830

NATIONAL PORTRAIT Artist Ralph E. W. Earl painted Jackson standing on the South Portico of the White House around 1836. Earl portrays the president with all the trappings of power, with Congress—represented by the Capitol—in the background.

JOHN C. CALHOUN

John C. Calhoun of South Carolina was one of Jackson's early supporters, helping to elect him in 1828. Calhoun and Jackson both wanted to see the country return to Jeffersonian principles—including, ironically, decentralized government—and rid Washington of the corruption of the political elite. However, over the years, a number of issues divided the men. The final break came when Jackson learned that Calhoun authored South Carolina's position on nullification. Jackson was furious. It was bad enough that a state would consider willfully violating federal law, but to have his own vice president leading the nullifiers was unthinkable. Calhoun resigned in December 1832.

BANK VETO After the bank veto, the Senate blocked Jackson's dismantling of the bank and censured Jackson's actions. Here, Henry Clay sews Jackson's mouth closed to represent the Senate's refusal to publish Jackson's official protest.

HENRY CLAY

Henry Clay was one of Andrew Jackson's chief opponents. Though the presidency eluded him three times, Clay had a celebrated political career as Speaker of the House of Representatives, secretary of state, and US senator. Clay played a pivotal role in Washington. He was a War Hawk in the early 1800s, encouraging the United States to declare war on Britain, and supported the Second Bank of the United States. Despite nearly always siding against Andrew Jackson, Clay stepped in during the nullification crisis with South Carolina, negotiating a tariff reduction compromise that placated South Carolina and kept Jackson from having to use force against the state.

BANK WAR

Like Thomas Jefferson before him, Andrew Jackson had long been suspicious of the Bank of the United States. In 1816, the United States Congress had chartered the private Second Bank of the United States to hold the country's money, make loans, and regulate currency. Bank profits benefited private stockholders, as well as the government, which owned stock in the bank. In its early years, the bank was riddled with corruption and poor financial management, creating economic hardship for the young nation. Under the direction of the bank's new president Nicholas Biddle, who took office in 1822, the bank's fortunes turned around. Yet Jackson and others still worried that a private institution had so much control over the country's economy.

In 1832, when there were four years left on the original charter of the Second Bank, Henry Clay introduced legislation to extend the bank's charter. Clay was once again running against Jackson for president, and knowing Jackson opposed the bank, Clay wanted to make it a campaign issue. Jackson responded by vetoing the legislation, declaring that the bank was unconstitutional and that it privileged "the rich and powerful" over ordinary "farmers, mechanics, and laborers."

Although Clay believed that voters would rally around the bank and its supporters out of fear it would fail, the American people overwhelmingly reelected Jackson in 1832. Jackson interpreted his victory as "the people's" mandate to destroy the powerful bank and replace it with a decentralized government banking system. Jackson pushed his banking plan through Congress, handicapping the bank in the meantime by ordering the removal of government deposits.

In response, the bank created an artificial economic panic by calling in many outstanding loans. The opposition-controlled Senate censured Jackson for removing the deposits without congressional authorization. Meanwhile, the old debate over liberty and power raged as Jackson, Congress, and the bank all accused each other of abusing their powers.

> ## Did You Know?
>
> Jackson kept a watchful eye over government spending. These controls and increased revenue enabled him to pay off the national debt in 1835, for the only time in US history.

ANTI-BANK TICKET
This ticket lists pro-Jackson candidates for the Maryland General Assembly in the 1832 election.

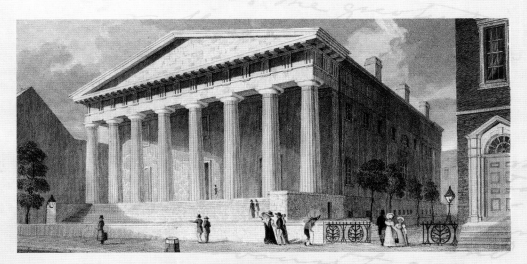

SECOND BANK OF THE UNITED STATES Located in Philadelphia, this impressive Greek Revival structure—designed by architect William Strickland in 1819—was the headquarters of the Second Bank of the United States.

LEGACY

Andrew Jackson is the only American president whose name defines an entire era of history. The "Age of Jackson" was a time of great change in America—economically, socially, and politically. Many of Jackson's countrymen feared this transformation, but others viewed it with great optimism.

Even today, Andrew Jackson is awash in a storm of controversy. His life is full of contradiction, much like the country he helped build. One of his earliest biographers, James Parton, called him "a democratic autocrat" and "an atrocious saint." Without fail, every generation of historians has reshaped and revised our understanding of Jackson and will no doubt continue to do so. The reason is simple: Andrew Jackson is inextricably woven into the fabric of America.

Though born in obscurity, Jackson rose to be president and squarely set the executive branch on equal footing with Congress in terms of its power and ability to shape law and policy. The result was indelible change in the government. Jackson also preserved and defended the Union against threats from nullifiers and secessionists.

Jackson fought hard to bring about a nation of "We the People" and give voice to all those he represented as president; however, this expansion of democracy did not include everyone. Slavery remained a pervasive part of American society, as did the continuing displacement of Native Americans. Opportunities for women and free blacks were still largely nonexistent.

Nevertheless, Jackson helped to inspire a uniquely American sense of promise and hope—establishing the idea that Americans can succeed through hard work and natural ability, not simply through unearned power and privilege.

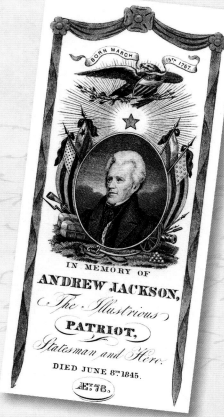

MEMORIAL RIBBON, 1845
Memorial ribbons were often printed upon the deaths of dignitaries.

HARRY S. TRUMAN

Harry Truman was sworn in as president of the United States on April 2, 1945, after the unexpected death of Franklin D. Roosevelt. Truman was an ardent admirer of Jackson, especially the strength of his presidency, his belief in the will of the people, and his unwavering commitment to speak out about issues of his time. Truman believed that he and Jackson were both outspoken men of the people. He commissioned a statue of Jackson to sit outside the courthouse in Kansas City, Missouri, during his term as presiding judge of Jackson County. When he was president, he presented a statue of Jackson to the courthouse in his hometown of Independence.

GENERAL JACKSON Although Jackson left the military in 1821, his earliest fame was achieved through military accomplishments. Even while president, Jackson preferred to be addressed as general. This title is on his tombstone.

"I thank God that my life has been spent in a land of liberty and that He has given me a heart to love my country with the affection of a son."
—ANDREW JACKSON, FAREWELL ADDRESS, MARCH 4, 1837

ASSASSINATION ATTEMPT
Richard Lawrence fired two shots at President Jackson at short range. Luckily, both guns misfired. Lawrence claimed Jackson killed his father and prevented his accession to the throne of England.

Did You Know?

The first assassination attempt on a sitting US president occurred on January 30, 1835, when Richard Lawrence attempted to shoot Andrew Jackson outside the Capitol building. Although Jackson believed that the Whig Party hired Lawrence to shoot him, there was no basis for his suspicion.

When Andrew Jackson left Washington for home on March 7, 1837, well-wishers lined his route, cheering for the man who had sacrificed much to give them a voice in Washington. Although he was no longer president, others still sought his counsel and support. From The Hermitage, Jackson kept an active correspondence with many people in Washington, offering his insight and advice. He also found great joy in spending time with his family and attending church.

TRUE HORSEMAN Andrew Jackson was passionate about horse racing and even kept racehorses at the White House.

THE HERMITAGE Andrew Jackson's home underwent extensive remodeling after a devastating 1834 fire. The renovations were completed about 1837 and echo the Greek Revival style employed at the White House.

ICONIC VIEW Artist Francis Strickland captured many details of The Hermitage correctly in 1856, including the cedar trees lining the drive and the tomb in the garden. However, the enslaved workers were unlikely to greet visitors in the road.

ANDREW JACKSON JR.

In 1808, the Jacksons took in one of the infant twins of Rachel's brother Severn Donelson and raised him as their own. They named him Andrew Jackson Jr. Although the reason for the adoption is unclear, Andrew Jr. and his twin, Thomas Jefferson Donelson, remained close all their lives. Andrew Jr. attended school at Davidson Academy and the University of Nashville. When Jackson became president, Andrew Jr. assumed management of the Hermitage farm. He married Sarah Yorke in 1831. They had five children, but only three survived into adulthood. The Hermitage remained in his family's care until 1889, when it became a museum.

THE HERMITAGE

In 1804, when Andrew Jackson purchased the Hermitage property, he could not possibly have known the path his life would take—through the South and into New Orleans and Florida, then on to the White House. But from the very beginning, Jackson was a man who dreamed big and worked with single-minded focus to transform his dreams into reality.

"Hermitage," simply defined, means a reclusive solitary retreat. Andrew Jackson's Hermitage was his escape from the world, but it was hardly solitary. A cotton plantation, The Hermitage was also the home of three generations of family members as well as over one hundred enslaved workers, making it a small village buzzing with constant activity—even when Jackson was in the White House.

On March 7, 1837, Jackson left Washington, DC, to return to The Hermitage for good. Jackson remained interested in politics and promoted several policies, including the annexation of Texas. He

died in his bedroom at The Hermitage on June 8, 1845, surrounded by loved ones. He was buried two days later in the Hermitage garden with nearly three thousand people in attendance.

His family carried on his hospitality after his death and, since 1889, generations of dedicated women and men have given their time and resources to keep The Hermitage open as a public museum. The Hermitage has welcomed tens of millions of visitors from around the world and is known for its research on and interpretation of slavery, as well as its award-winning exhibit about Jackson's life. In addition, original furniture, wallpaper, and family possessions give visitors a glimpse of what life was like for the family during Andrew Jackson's retirement.

THE friends and acquaintance of GEN. ANDREW JACKSON are invited to attend his Funeral at the Hermitage, on to-morrow (Tuesday) morning at 11 o'clock. Divine service by the Rev. Dr. Edgar. His death took place last evening at 6 o'clock.
Nashville, Monday, June 9, 1845.

JACKSON'S FUNERAL NOTICE In Jackson's time, families hand-delivered notices of deaths and funerals. Nearly three thousand mourners attended Jackson's funeral.

FINAL RESTING PLACE Andrew and Rachel Jackson were laid to rest in this Greek Revival style tomb.

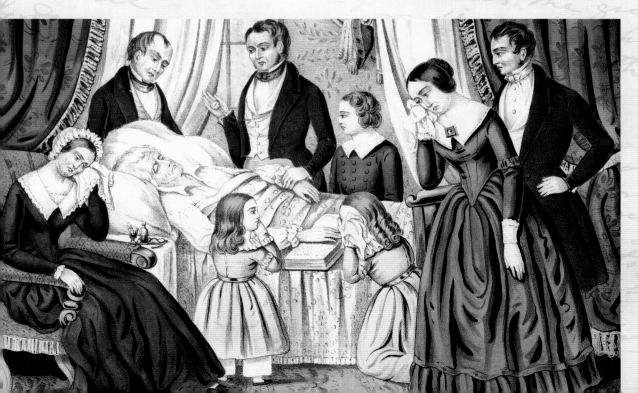

SLOW DECLINE Jackson suffered a slow decline before his death. He passed away surrounded by family on June 8, 1845. This print omits enslaved servants George and Hannah, who also watched.

IN DETAIL Few images exist of The Hermitage that Rachel Jackson would have known. This image, a detail of *The Tennessee Gentleman* by Ralph E. W. Earl (shown opposite), depicts The Hermitage as a red brick house with a white porch, surrounded by a white fence and formal garden.

IN HIS TIME

In 1834, a fire heavily damaged the Hermitage mansion. When the house was rebuilt, the entrance façade was transformed into a Greek temple. Inside, the builders reused the outmoded Federal-style woodwork in the more private family bedrooms. In the public rooms, they added Greek Revival–style mantels and woodwork. New French wallpaper was hung, and the destroyed furnishings were replaced with Philadelphia classical-style pieces. When completed in 1837, The Hermitage was perhaps the most fashionable house in Tennessee.

HERMITAGE MANSION Andrew Jackson's Greek Revival mansion became as well known as the man himself.

TENNESSEE GENTLEMAN This circa 1830 portrait depicts Andrew Jackson standing in front of the original Hermitage mansion. Jackson was proud to own this expansive plantation, which was in stark contrast to his backcountry childhood.

HOME OF THE PEOPLE'S PRESIDENT

BECKON BOOKS

The mission of the Andrew Jackson Foundation is to preserve the home of Andrew Jackson, create educational opportunities, and inspire citizenship through learning about his life and unique impact on American history. The nonprofit Andrew Jackson Foundation, originally named the Ladies' Hermitage Association, operates The Hermitage daily. Its aim is to increase the public's understanding of the complex life and times of Andrew Jackson, to discuss its relationship to events of today, and to inspire citizenship and pride in our nation. The Andrew Jackson Foundation endeavors to accomplish this through preservation, interpretation, exhibition, education, research, and publication.

Andrew Jackson's Hermitage
4580 Rachel's Lane
Nashville, TN 37076
615-889-2941
www.thehermitage.com

ISBN: 978-1-935442-60-8
Printed in China
10 9 8 7 6 5 4 3 2 1

Andrew Jackson: The People's President was developed by Beckon Books in cooperation with the Andrew Jackson Foundation. Beckon develops and publishes custom books for leading cultural attractions, corporations, and nonprofit organizations. Beckon Books is an imprint of Southwestern Publishing Group, Inc., 2451 Atrium Way, Nashville, Tennessee, 37214. Southwestern Publishing Group, Inc., is a wholly owned subsidiary of Southwestern, Inc., Nashville, Tennessee.

Christopher G. Capen, President, Southwestern
    Publishing Group
Betsy Holt, Publisher, Beckon Books
Vicky Shea, Senior Art Director
Kristin Connelly, Managing Editor
Jennifer Benson, Proofreader
www.beckonbooks.com | 800-358-0560